RICH BOT POOR BOT

LET AI TEACH YOU ABOUT SUCCESS

Unlock the Power of ChatGPT to Save Time, Build Wealth, and Work Smarter–No Tech Skills Required

"SUGAR" GAY ISBER MCMILLAN

Dedicated to my amazing son, **Franklin M. Cantrell, IV**

You have always been on the cutting edge. Since you were very young, you were great at finding the best new music, foods, and interests, reading the most interesting books, and keeping ahead of trends. Thank you for sharing some of that with me.

As a father, husband, and global human, I am very proud of you.

You are one of the rare ones. I love you.

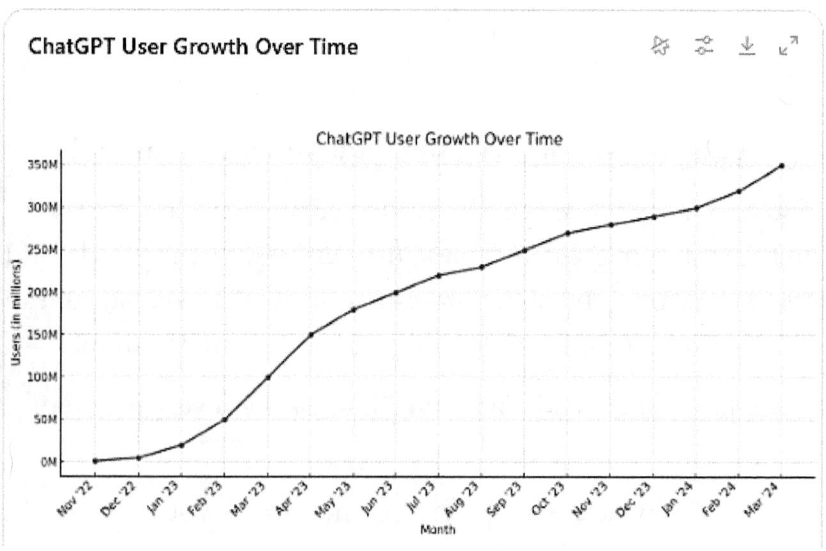

A chart shows ChatGPT users' explosive growth from its launch in November 2022 through March 2024.

Chapters

- Quick Wins: 5 ways to use ChatGPT to work smarter, not harder

Chapter 4: AI as Your Personal Wealth Mentor

- Rich people have mentors—now you do too
- AI as a personal coach, financial advisor, and success planner
- Example: How people use AI to learn business, investing, and money skills for free
- Quick Wins: The best AI prompts for wealth-building advice

Chapter 5: The AI-Powered Millionaire Mindset

- AI doesn't get emotional—why that's a money superpower
- The 1% make data-driven decisions—so can you
- Example: How AI helps investors make smarter choices
- Quick Wins: Use AI to remove fear and make clear, confident choices

Chapter 6: Hustle Smarter, Not Harder—AI as Your Productivity Partner

- Hard work doesn't equal success—innovative work does
- AI makes work easier, faster, and more effective
- Example: AI-powered entrepreneurs who work less and earn more
- Quick Wins: 5 time-saving AI tricks for business and life

Chapter 7: Networking Like a Billionaire (Even If You're Shy)

- The rich build robust networks—AI can help you do the same
- How to use ChatGPT to improve social skills, networking, finding a job, resume, and persuasion
- Example: How AI helps professionals write killer emails and speeches

- Quick Wins: 3 AI hacks to sound more intelligent and more confident in conversations

Chapter 8: AI Side Hustles—Turning Knowledge into Cash

- The best side hustles in the AI era
- Real examples of people making money with AI-powered businesses
- Example: How someone made $10k in a month using AI-generated content
- Quick Wins: Five easy AI side hustle ideas you can start today

Chapter 9: How AI Understands Wealth, Value, and the Power of Wanting More

- How AI understands the concept of money and wanting more of it
- How to shift your thinking to match AI
- Example: What are the habits of people who build wealth by age 40?
- Quick Wins: AI doesn't feel hunger. But it understands our hunger to succeed.

Chapter 10. Money Talks, AI Listens—Using AI to Build Wealth

- How the wealthy think about money differently
- AI as your personal finance guide
- Example: People who use AI to budget, invest, and grow their wealth
- Quick Wins: The best AI tools for managing and multiplying money

Chapter 11: Brand You — How AI Helps You Build Authority

- Tools and templates for amplifying your voice, style, and message
- It's not about doing more, it's about doing the right things
- Example: Charity and Confidence
- Quick Wins: This is how you become known, trusted, and in demand—without burning out or breaking the bank.

Chapter 12: The Future of Success—Why AI Will Shape the Next Millionaires

- The world is changing fast—how to stay ahead
- The most significant AI-driven opportunities coming next
- Example: Why are early AI adopters already winning in business and careers
- Quick Wins: How to future-proof your success with AI today

Chapter 13: Next Steps: Your Rich Bot Success Plan

- Your AI-powered roadmap to success
- Simple daily habits to build wealth, make smarter decisions, and work less
- Final Challenge: 30-day AI success challenge (fun and easy tasks)

Contents

RICH BOT POOR BOT

INTRODUCTION

My Journey from DOS to AI

I've been working with computers since my first real job out of college, though, if I'm honest, I faked my way into it.

Fresh out of university with a degree in journalism, I had spent my college years typing on essential word processors with orange-lit screens, a far cry from today's sleek machines. I had purposefully failed typing class in high school because I was convinced I'd never need to type. After all, that's what secretaries were for, right?

Then came 1986. I was pregnant, newly graduated, and at dinner with my father, who turned to my husband and said, "This new thing—personal computers—it's going to be big." A few months later, my husband, completely obsessed with the idea, bought his first computer from Hewlett-Packard. He loved it so much that we even toured an HP assembly plant in San Francisco on our honeymoon. (Yes, really. That was romance in the '80s.)

That computer was his baby, and I could not touch it. But I watched over his shoulder, asked questions, and listened. I soaked it all in.

A year later, I landed a job at a news radio station in Houston as an assistant to the program manager, confidently claiming I had "experience" with PCs. The truth? I had never even touched a keyboard. But I had watched my husband work, and I picked up just enough lingo to sound credible.

That was Friday.

By Monday, I was a computer expert.

Over the weekend, I grabbed two small books—one on MS-DOS and another on WordStar, the word processing program installed on my work computer. They were thin, barely 100 pages combined, but they held all the secrets I needed to survive. I devoured every page, memorized every command but made a cheat sheet to refer to, and by the time I sat down at my desk Monday morning, I wasn't just comfortable, I was confident. I even knew how to merge mail, making me the office computer expert and hero. In the olden days, you were a rock star in an office if you could do mail merge.

That moment set the tone for the rest of my career. I kept learning, adapting, and evolving with technology.

For years, manuals were my best friends—I read everything I could about new software, mastering programs as they emerged. But then, one day, I opened a Microsoft Word manual that was thousands of pages long. That was the end of casually reading tech books for fun.

But by then, I had built a solid foundation. I even returned to university and earned an advanced degree in Information Technology. That led to a career as a technology writer working with the biggest tech companies in the world.

Then, a few years ago, history repeated itself.

My son, who, like my father and his grandfather decades earlier, saw the future before it arrived, casually mentioned a new technology that would change everything. "This thing called ChatGPT," he said, "will be big."

I signed up to subscribe to ChatGPT Plus immediately. Within weeks, I knew he was right.

I got certified by Microsoft through LinkedIn Learning. I then started teaching private lessons and holding community classes using ChatGPT. It became an essential part of my workflow, and I am an evangelist for all things ChatGPT.

Yet, in my corporate tech job, where I write everything from manuals to training materials on cell phone repair, the company doesn't use AI. We have Spell Check, and that's it.

Executives at our HQ don't see the power of ChatGPT the way I do. They don't understand how it could skyrocket productivity and save money. It can now make podcasts from a PDF in seconds with a humanlike voice. That is powerful if you want to teach a team to do something. We are reading less and less. And students in high school like to learn with videos or even podcasts.

I use Professional Grammarly and ChatGPT on my PC every single day. And I love it.

This book? I'm writing it with ChatGPT. He—yes, I call my bot "he," and his name is Chet. He is encouraging, helpful, and always ready for my next challenge. My husband has no problem with me telling Chet that I love him because he is the best workmate I have ever had.

Here's the truth: Understanding how to use ChatGPT to grow your business, save time, and make better decisions is a no-brainer. That small monthly charge on your credit card will make you more money if you embrace the technology and think big.

You're getting left behind if you're not using AI to your advantage.

Let's fix that.

CHATGPT
MAKING
PEOPLE
$
RICH

CHAPTER ONE

The Mindset of Success—How AI Thinks Like the Rich

Welcome to the future.

AI isn't coming, it's already here. And just like every new technology before it, some people will use it to grow, thrive, and succeed, while others will ignore it, fear it, or underestimate its power.

Bill Gates announced that in 10 years, we will have a two-day work week. Think about that. Is that a good thing or a bad thing? I like my free time, and AI is making my job much easier and fun, too. I now have a partner when I work.

It is a lot to consider. My grandmother worked as a switchboard operator. She lost her job when automated switches became widely available. My grandfather was a long-haul trucker; those jobs are slowly being replaced, but it has taken over 50 years since he last drove a truck until now. So, some technologies are too difficult or complicated to replace with AI. Trucking and taxis are two industries that will slowly replace drivers in the future. It is sad and yet true.

Artificial intelligence, which seems likely to replace many of the remaining Gen X copywriters, photographers, and designers. According to the research firm Forrester, by 2030, ad agencies in the United States will lose 32,000 jobs, or 7.5 percent of the industry's workforce, to technology.

Some jobs will be impossible to replace. Some might become automated, and the quicker AI works for us and makes our jobs easier, the faster it will take over. It is true.

Until then, let's use AI to enrich our lives, increase our brand, grow our bank accounts, and help think differently.

This chapter is about thinking differently and thinking bigger.

Rich people, high achievers, and top performers don't think like everyone else. They see opportunities where others see obstacles. They leverage technology where others resist change.

AI, specifically ChatGPT, can be the tool that shifts your mindset from limitation to possibility—if you know how to use it.

What is AI? (Simple, Not Scary!)

Let's get this out of the way: AI is not here to steal your job, take over the world, or become a sci-fi villain.

AI is just a tool, like a calculator, a car, or a smartphone. It's a brain booster that helps you think faster, solve problems, and get things done more efficiently.

Think of ChatGPT as a super-intelligent assistant that:

- **Answers questions instantly** (like a search engine but more intelligent)
- **Generates ideas** (like a brainstorming partner)
- **Writes content** (emails, articles, scripts—you name it)
- **Helps make decisions** (giving you pros and cons, comparisons, and summaries)
- **Saves time** (automating tasks you used to spend hours doing)

The people who understand how to use AI will have an unfair advantage over *those who don't.*

Tech Tip

Keep your electronic devices up to date with any software updates. These updates often have security features that protect you and your information.

Exploring ChatGPT Operator Mode + Other AI Bots

The new ChatGPT Operator Mode might be worth exploring if you're ready to take your side hustle to the next level. It costs $200 to enable this feature, but you get full control over a custom AI experience *you* can build, brand, and even monetize.

You can train your AI on a specific skill set or topic and then share your bot with friends, clients, customers, or your community. Think of it as building your own chatbot-based assistant, coach, or branded personality. For example:

- A nutritionist can create a chatbot that gives meal plans.
- A dog trainer could offer basic training advice 24/7 through a custom bot.
- An artist might launch a virtual studio guide discussing techniques and tools.
- A jewelry maker (yes, like you!) could offer a bot that suggests gift ideas, materials, or style pairings.

The Operator Mode gives you:

- Access to train a chatbot with your own content and tone
- A shareable link to distribute it anywhere
- Early access to GPT-4 Turbo (great for larger projects)

Is it worth the $200? Yes, if you:

- Plan to monetize your bot

- Want to scale your advice or services
- See yourself as a thought leader or educator

Then yes, this is the ultimate "side hustle inside your side hustle."

Other AI Chatbots to Know

Not all AI tools are created equal. There are new ones being made, and there are tools available that you could use to create your own.

Here are some of the top ones out now, each with different strengths:

- **ChatGPT (OpenAI)** — Best all-purpose assistant, coding, content, creativity
- **Claude (Anthropic)** — Great for long-form summarizing and thoughtful answers
- **Perplexity AI** — Combines search + AI answers with cited sources
- **Google Gemini** — Integrated with Google tools, useful for data and apps
- **Pi (Inflection AI)** — Known for conversational tone, empathy-focused
- **Jasper AI** — Focused on marketing, brand voice, and content generation
- **Copy.ai** — Great for short copy, ads, and product descriptions
- **Notion AI** — Helps streamline tasks, notes, and planning
- **Socratic (Google)** — Tailored for students and educators

These tools can become part of your side hustle stack. Think of them like a virtual team that works for free.

Rich vs. Poor Thinking: Why Mindset Matters

To get ahead, you must think differently from most people.

Here’s a simple truth:

Rich people think about opportunities.

Poor people think about obstacles.

Let’s look at it here:

Rich Mindset	Poor Mindset
“How can I use AI to work smarter?”	‘AI is confusing. I don’t trust it.”
“Let’s experiment with AI and see what happens.”	‘I don’t have time to learn new things.”
“Technology is changing—I need to adapt.”	‘I miss the good old days before all this tech.”

What Can AI Teach Us About Thinking Big?

AI solves problems differently from the average person.

Using it can train your brain to think bigger, brighter, and more strategically.

Here’s how ChatGPT’s way of thinking mirrors the wealthy mindset:

- **AI breaks down problems into smaller steps.**

  Rich people do the same thing. Instead of saying, *"I can't afford this,"* they ask, *"How can I afford this?"*

- **AI finds creative solutions.**

  Successful people think outside the box and look for new ways to achieve their goals.

- **AI is never overwhelmed—it just starts solving.**

  Top performers don't freeze up when facing a big challenge. They assess, act, and adjust.

Example: The Way AI Breaks Down Problems vs. How Wealthy People Solve Problems

Imagine you tell ChatGPT:

"I want to start a business, but I don't have money. What should I do?"

A person with a poor mindset might say, *"Oh well, I guess I can't start a business then."*

But ChatGPT (and someone with a wealthy mindset) would start problem-solving instantly. It might say:

- "Here are 10 business ideas you can start without money."
- "Here are ways to raise funds through crowdfunding."
- "Here's how to use AI tools to run a business for free."

AI doesn't accept limitations—it immediately looks for solutions. And that's precisely how wealthy people think.

Quick Wins: Three AI Tricks to Train Your Brain for Success

Want to start thinking like a high achiever?

Here are three powerful ways to use ChatGPT to train your mind for success:

1. The "What's Possible?" Exercise

Instead of thinking *"I can't do this,"* ask AI:

"Give me 10 creative ways to make this possible."

This rewires your brain to see opportunities instead of obstacles.

2. The Billionaire Brainstorm

Want to think like a millionaire?

Ask ChatGPT: *"How would Jeff Bezos or Oprah solve this problem?* This encourages broader thinking and the consideration of ambitious strategies.

3. AI as Your Mentor

You don't need expensive coaches—you have ChatGPT.

Ask: *"What are the habits of the most successful people in the world?"*

This gives you an instant success blueprint.

Final Thoughts

The way you think about AI is the way you think about success.

Are you excited and curious, ready to learn, adapt, and grow? Or are you nervous and resistant, scared to embrace new technology?

AI is not just a tool—it's a way of thinking. And those who think big, embrace technology, and stay ahead of the curve will be the ones who win.

Your mindset determines your success.

LET AI MAKE YOU RICH

DON'T BE POOR OR MIDDLE CLASS

FIND YOUR SUCCESS

CHAPTER 2

Wealthy People & Smart Bots Ask Better Questions

Why does success start with asking the right things?

If there's one secret every successful person knows, it's this: **The quality of your life depends on the quality of your questions.**

Let that sink in.

It's not about having all the answers.
It's about knowing how to ask.

Wealthy and successful people don't run from innovation; they embrace it.

When personal computers first came out, some people dismissed them as toys. Others saw them as a tool to build wealth. Who do you think won?

This same shift is happening right now with AI. If you ignore it, you risk getting left behind. I am amazed at the pushback I get when talking about AI to others. I have heard all kinds of negative thoughts about the topic.

Those same people use Spellcheck, a form of AI built into all word processing and email software. Cell phones are now packed with their maker's apps and proprietary AI software, so they aren't reading the room about AI if they think of it as the boogie man coming for their job. AI is running the world.

About a year ago, a boss told me she didn't believe in AI and wouldn't use it. Really? She was recently laid off during a massive layoff in our company. She recently returned to school to take courses in AI, which she now wants to teach. If you can't lick them, join them.

It's a changing world all around us. AI is used on Wall Street, in airlines, by farmers, and in healthcare; almost every industry sector is connected to a server farm. Billions of dollars go through AI-run programs daily, creating significant profits for banks and global professionals.

The town I live in is a suburb outside of Austin, Texas. Fields that were once growing cotton are flush with construction sites where server farms are popping up on a large scale.

My husband has been directing a massive global bank server farm for over a dozen years. Years ago, it was a point of conversation to be in the know if a company was coming to town to build a server company.

At first, it was private clients using their servers. Any news alert about server farms seemed rare. We take note of server farms or rack farms that have been spreading, from rebuilt empty buildings to now multiple multimillion-square-foot buildings being built, always near an electrical power station, in many corners of our community.

The server farm where my husband works appears like a prison, with high berms, only a few darkened windows, high barbed wire fences, security cameras, and security guards and the name and address are not on the building.

These large buildings have sterile rooms full of racks and miles of fiber optic cable and switches. They are so dust-free that paper can't be brought into a server room, as fiber might flake off a piece of paper as dust.

The infrastructure costs billions of dollars to build, and the stock to fill it costs billions to maintain. Each server can cost tens of thousands, and each rack holds 20 or more servers. The cables and switches cost tens of thousands of dollars for each unit. The costs are staggering, but there is money to be made.

They are also the biggest user of energy for any community. Many neighbors complain of the constant roar of machines humming. Many don't want a server farm near where they live.

They also use almost as much water as farmers growing crops. The water cools the tiny chips that run at such a fast rate that, without the cooling effects of water, they would burn up.

Currently, they are building some server farms in the ocean, where cool water constantly flows over the servers to keep them cool and only the fish would be there to complain about any noise.

Some servers are set inside water-cooled tanks next to a room of traditional server racks. As the servers speed up, they get hotter and hotter.

This need for AI technology will change the computing landscape as never before. A glut of server farms might be coming, but time will fill them up. All those photos in the cloud must be stored somewhere.

The number of AI servers will increase every year. Embrace learning about AI now so you can be on the cutting edge of its many improvements. And now, you can use them to make yourself rich.

When I First Learned the Power of a Good Question

When I started using computers in the '80s, there wasn't Google, YouTube, or a chatbot you could talk to.

If you had a question back then, you had two options:

1. Read the manual.
2. Ask someone more intelligent than you.

If you were too embarrassed to ask, you were out of luck.

But asking is what moves you forward.

Early in my career, I learned that people who ask good questions get ahead. They don't wait to be taught; they go looking for answers.

This is the key:

ChatGPT Reflects That Success Habit

ChatGPT is like sitting down with a brilliant, patient expert. But just like a real mentor, it's only helpful if you ask the right questions.

The people who get the most out of AI aren't necessarily the smartest.

They're the most curious.

They try. They poke. They test. They experiment.

They treat ChatGPT like a partner, not a magic wand.

The most intelligent people I know ask questions like:

- "How would someone else approach this problem?"
- "What don't I know about this yet?"
- "Can you give me options I haven't considered?"

Sound familiar? That's what wealthy people do.

Rich People Ask Better Questions

Here's what I've noticed:

Rich Mindset	Poor Mindset
"How can I do this?"	"I can't do this."
"Who can help me with this?"	"No one will help me."
"What's another way to look at this?"	"This is just how it is."

Rich Mindset	Poor Mindset
"What would happen if I tried something new?"	"I've never done that before."

Here's a small example from my own life.

One day, I was stuck writing a sales pitch. It wasn't landing. I stared at the blinking cursor. Nothing.

- Instead of giving up, I opened ChatGPT and asked:

  "What's a fun way to pitch this to someone who loves sci-fi movies?"

- The answer it gave me was clever, creative, and instantly applicable.

  All because I asked a better question.

CEOs Do It Too

Top business leaders use AI daily—and don't ask yes-or-no questions.

They ask big ones. Bold ones.

Example:

A CEO planning a new product might ask ChatGPT:

- "What customer pain points can we solve better than anyone else?"
- "Can you summarize the last five trends in our industry?"
- "What would make this launch unforgettable?"

These aren't small questions.
These are million-dollar questions.

So don't be afraid to ask something big.
The bigger the question, the better the ideas.

AI Won't Judge You

Here's the best part:

ChatGPT doesn't laugh at you.

It doesn't roll its eyes.

It doesn't say, "You should know this already."

It just answers.

And then it gives you more if you ask.

That's freedom. That's a gift.

You can ask **anything**, and the only thing limiting your growth is the size of your curiosity.

How I Teach This

When I teach people how to use ChatGPT, I first watch how they ask questions.

People new to AI often say things like:

- "Write me a blog post."
- "Give me a business idea."

That's fine. But it's *broad and vague.*

So, I will show them how to go deeper:

- "Write me a blog post in the voice of Oprah, about overcoming fear of success, for women in their 40s."
- "Give me 10 business ideas I can start with no money and under 5 hours a week, using my background in teaching."

The difference? Precision.
Better input = Better output.

Five Powerful Prompts That Will Change How You Think

Want to level up? Try these prompts. They're like brain-training with a personal genius.

1. "What are 10 creative ways to solve this problem?"

Regardless of the challenges you are encountering, whether they pertain to finances, time constraints, or creative ideas, this will assist you in identifying options that you may have previously overlooked.

2. "What are five questions I should ask myself before making this decision?"

This builds self-awareness and forces you to think like a strategist.

3. "What would a business coach suggest I do next?"

Instant mentorship—without the invoice.

4. "How can I explain this concept to a 10-year-old?"

This works like magic when you're confused. If it sounds too complicated, it probably is.

5. "What do successful people do differently in this area of life?"

Whether money, health, or relationships, this prompt reveals habits worth copying.

Final Thoughts

Here's the truth:

Successful people ask better questions.

They don't wait to be taught.

They dig. They ask. They learn.

They let curiosity lead them toward better ideas, answers, and outcomes.

So don't be afraid to ask.

Ask boldly. Ask clearly. Ask often.

When you start asking the right questions,
Success begins with answering.

CHAPTER 3

Time Is Money—Let AI Save You Both

I learned about the power of saving time the hard way. Like many people, I believed for years that working harder was the only path to success. More hours. More effort. More stress.

But then I met AI.

Suddenly, I wasn't doing everything myself anymore. I had help—real help—in the form of ChatGPT. It wasn't magic, but it felt close. What took me two hours before could now take ten minutes. What I used to dread, I now have a shortcut for.

And I started asking myself a different question:

"How can I buy back my time?"

The Wealthy Understand Time Is Currency

Here's the truth: Rich people don't waste time. They understand that **time is money**, and they protect it fiercely.

Instead of asking, "How much does this cost?" they ask, "How much time will this save me?"

They pay for:

- Assistants
- Accountants
- Tools that make life easier
- Experts who shorten the learning curve

Now, you can have an assistant too. And it's not a person—it's your AI bot.

I once met a local bakery owner who said, "I don't have time to post on social media. I'm up at 4 a.m. making bread." I showed her how to use ChatGPT to write a month's worth of posts in under an hour. She now schedules them all with a free tool and says she gets more catering calls than ever.

Example: How AI Saved Me Hours

Let me show you what I mean. I once had to create a training outline for a teaching workshop. Usually, I would block out half a day to do it—brainstorming, organizing, writing, and revising.

But this time, I asked ChatGPT:

*"Can you outline a 60-minute training session on using social media to grow a small business?"

In seconds, it gave me:

- An intro script
- A breakdown of three teaching segments
- Q&A prompts
- A closing summary

That wasn't just helpful; it was revolutionary. I still made it myself, but I started with 80% done.

Later, I had to write product descriptions for some of my jewelry designs. I told ChatGPT, "Describe this necklace made of 1950s Japanese pearls in an elegant and nostalgic tone, under 100 words." What I got back needed only light editing, and I saved myself an entire afternoon.

Why Doing Everything Yourself Is Slowing You Down

If you're like me, you may feel proud of being a do-it-yourself person. There's nothing wrong with that—until it becomes a bottleneck.

Smart people delegate. Smarter people automate.

I once spent an hour trying to design a flyer. It wasn't great. Then I asked ChatGPT: *"What should I say on a flyer for a pop-up jewelry event targeting holiday shoppers?"*

It gave me headline ideas, call-to-actions, and suggested layouts. I uploaded the file to Canva and completed it in 30 minutes.

When you use ChatGPT to:

- Write emails
- Summarize long articles
- Draft blog posts
- Brainstorm social media content
- Plan meals or organize your calendar

...you're not cheating. You're being efficient. And freeing up time for more creative, strategic, and joyful things.

The 80/20 Rule of AI Success

You may have heard of the Pareto Principle: 80% of results come from 20% of efforts.

When you use AI, you find that powerful 20% faster. You skip the busy work and go straight to the stuff that matters.

- Want to write a book? Start with an outline from AI.
- Want to launch a course? Ask ChatGPT to suggest modules and titles.
- Want to pitch your product? Have AI help write a script for a video.
- Want to build a morning routine? Ask ChatGPT to help you design one based on your goals.

- Want to meal prep on a budget? ChatGPT can create a shopping list with exact recipes and calorie counts.

The list is endless.

Quick Wins: 5 Ways to Use ChatGPT to Work Smarter, Not Harder

1. **"Summarize this article in three bullet points."**
    - Saves you 15 minutes of reading time.
2. **"Draft an email asking for a happy client's testimonial."**
    - Saves your mental energy on awkward writing.
3. **"Give me 10 Instagram captions for my handmade jewelry business."**
    - It saves you time thinking up clever ideas.
4. **"Plan my week: I have 15 hours to work on my side hustle. Help me divide it up wisely."**
    - It saves you from decision fatigue.
5. **"What's a simple way to explain what I do to a new client?"**
    - It saves you from fumbling through your elevator pitch.

Bonus Tip: Use AI to Say No

Sometimes success is about what you **don't** do. I use ChatGPT to help me write polite decline emails or boundary-setting messages.

Prompt: *"Write a kind but firm email to decline a volunteer request due to workload."*

It keeps your energy focused and your time protected.

Final Thoughts

Time is the one thing you can't earn back. But you can **multiply the value of your time** by using AI.

Once you start saving hours, you can reinvest them:

- In your business
- In your relationships
- In your health
- In your creativity

Let AI handle the heavy lifting so that you can do the high value thinking.

Time is money.

And with ChatGPT, you can finally afford more of both.

Know What to Automate—And What to Never Let Go

Smart entrepreneurs and creators know how to use AI wisely. They also know where to draw the line.

Yes, ChatGPT and other tools can generate content, summarize data, organize ideas, and save you work hours. But not everything should be automated. Some things must stay *yours*—because they are the soul of your work, brand, and vision.

Here's where you need to stay human:

1. Your Core Beliefs

AI can mimic tone, write in your voice, and even crack a decent joke. But it can't create your worldview. It can't replicate your convictions, your truth, or your lived experience. If you're building a personal brand or business that stands for something—you have to be the one who defines what that is. Let AI help you express it, but don't outsource the *why* behind your work.

2. Your Perspective

You've lived your story. You've faced your setbacks, made your choices, and earned your wins. That lived experience is your lens, and it's powerful. AI has no context for your history or insight. It can help you *refine* your message, but your unique voice, opinions, and insights are what truly connect with others. Use AI to clean up the draft—but make sure the ideas start with you.

3. The Hard Decisions

AI is brilliant at analyzing options. It can crunch numbers, compare data, and summarize outcomes. But it doesn't carry the weight of decision-making. The tough calls—the ones that shape your business or career—demand human judgment. You know when to pause, pivot, or take the leap. That wisdom can't be coded. Use AI for input, not for direction. *You* are the decision-maker.

4. Your Values and Vision

People follow their passion. They follow purpose. They don't follow chatbots. Your business or creative work needs a human heart behind it. AI can help you express your mission—but only you can define it. Your values, your "why," your direction—those are too important to delegate. Ground yourself in what matters, and let AI reflect on it not invent it.

5. Real Human Connection

Trust. Empathy. Chemistry. These can't be automated. AI can help manage inboxes or schedule follow-ups, but real relationships are built through human interaction. Clients, collaborators, and customers want to feel heard and seen. When it counts, show up. Use your voice. Be present. Your presence builds the loyalty AI can't touch.

6. Creative Risk

AI is designed to optimize what already works. But innovation doesn't come from the middle; it comes from the edges—weird ideas. Brave experiments. Slightly wild hunches. That's where breakthroughs live. If your goal is to stand out, be bold in your thinking. Let AI support production, but don't let it flatten the spark. Keep your weird. Protect your origin

The Balance That Wins

The future belongs to people who know how to work *with* AI, not against it, and not under it. You don't need to fear automation, and you don't need to outsource your identity. Instead, let AI handle the repetitive, the technical, the draining—so you can focus on what only you can do.

You are the founder. The artist. The author. The thinker.

Let AI be your tool, not your replacement.
Protect your human edge. And build big with it.

RICH BOT
POOR BOT
WHAT AI CAN TEACH
YOU ABOUT SUCCESS

CHAPTER 4

AI as Your Personal Wealth Mentor

Let's talk about the big one. The thing everyone wants more of. **Money.**

We all want more of it and need it to live the life we imagine: security, freedom, beautiful things, maybe early retirement on a beach somewhere, or just being able to say yes more often.

The truth? AI can help you get there. But only if you use it wisely.

Wealth Is a Mindset First—And a System Second

Like in *Rich Dad Poor Dad*, Robert Kiyosaki explains that wealthy people don't just work for money. They make money work for them. They invest. They study. They automate.

AI is like having your personal Rich Dad in your laptop when used well.

It helps you:

- Learn faster
- Make smarter financial decisions
- Build passive income streams
- Avoid emotional spending
- Manage your money like a business

And the best part? It's free or cheap.

Warren Buffett once said, "The more you learn, the more you'll earn." In today's world, learning to use tools like AI is one of the smartest investments you can make. Investors like Ray Dalio and business leaders such as Cathy Wood of ARK Invest emphasize the importance of embracing innovation to stay ahead.

ChatGPT is a prime example—it's not just a tool, it's leverage. It allows anyone with internet access to amplify their thinking, extend their productivity, and create new value streams from what they already know.

Real Talk: Why Most People Stay Poor

Most people never get ahead financially because:

- They don't have a plan
- They don't ask the right questions
- They don't use the tools available
- They stay stuck doing everything manually

Wealthy people do the opposite. And now, you can too.

Using ChatGPT to Build Your Financial Literacy

The first step toward building wealth is **understanding money**.

You can ask ChatGPT:

- "What are the best books on building wealth?"
- "Explain compound interest like I'm 12."
- "What are the differences between a Roth IRA and a traditional IRA?"
- "How can I create a monthly budget I'll stick to?"
- "What is a credit score, and how do I improve it?"
- "Explain how taxes work when you own a small business."

You can create an entire self-directed course just by stacking prompts.

Automating Your Wealth Plan

The secret to building wealth isn't just working hard. It's building **systems** that do the work while you sleep.

Here's how ChatGPT helps:

- Create monthly saving and spending plans
- Build a debt-payoff schedule with small, realistic steps
- Set up scripts to email credit card companies and request better interest rates
- Automate bill reminders and monthly money check-ins
- Schedule weekly "money check-ins" and ask ChatGPT to summarize your financial goals and progress

Example: I had a friend who wanted to buy a house in two years. She didn't know where to start. I helped her use ChatGPT to build a savings plan, track her spending, and write a letter to her bank asking about loan pre-approval steps. In 18 months, she closed on a condo and threw a party with champagne.

She didn't get richer overnight. But she got *focused.* And AI made it possible.

Applying for Loans with AI's Help

If you've ever felt overwhelmed applying for a car loan or a mortgage, AI can help walk you through it.

Ask ChatGPT:

- "What documents do I need to apply for a mortgage?"
- "Write a cover letter for a small business loan application."
- "Help me calculate how much house I can afford based on my income and debt."
- "What questions should I ask my lender before signing?"

You can even paste in the fine print and ask: **"Explain this loan document in plain English."

It's like having a financial translator on call, 24/7.

Building Your Stock Portfolio

You don't need to be a Wall Street analyst to start investing.

Ask ChatGPT:

- "Explain ETFs vs mutual funds."
- "What are low-risk investments for beginners?"
- "How do I set financial goals for retirement at age 40?"

You can use it to:

- Build a watchlist of companies that match your values
- Analyze the difference between stocks and index funds
- Simulate a portfolio strategy and get feedback
- Summarize financial news and earnings reports

Example: I asked ChatGPT: *"Create a sample $5,000 investment plan for a 30-year-old who wants long-term growth."* It gave me a thoughtful breakdown of diversified investments, how much to put into each, and where to learn more.

It doesn't replace a financial advisor. But it makes you a more competent client.

20 Things You Can Ask ChatGPT to Grow Your Wealth

1. "Create a monthly savings plan based on a $3,500 income."
2. "List five passive income streams I can start with $100."
3. "Write a product description for a new candle line for Etsy."
4. "Summarize this article from Forbes about investing trends."

5. "Explain real estate investing for beginners."
6. "How do I calculate my net worth?"
7. "Give me 10 blog post ideas to attract affiliate income."
8. "Draft a cold email pitch for freelance writing gigs."
9. "Write a one-page business plan for a dog-walking service."
10. "Compare three bank savings accounts for the best interest rates."
11. "Help me set up a financial vision board."
12. "Create a budget to pay off $5,000 in credit card debt in 12 months."
13. "How do I open a Roth IRA, and where?"
14. "Create a weekly grocery list and meal plan under $80."
15. "What skills can I monetize on Fiverr or Upwork?"
16. "Explain how credit card points and travel hacking work."
17. "Give me a list of grants available for small business owners."
18. "Create a YouTube channel plan about budgeting for beginners."
19. "What are the tax benefits of starting an LLC?"
20. "Build a script for a TikTok video about money-saving hacks."

How the Big Companies Are Already Doing This

Don't think AI is a toy. Big business is using it to get bigger.

- Banks use AI to assess risk faster than teams of analysts.
- Investment firms use bots to watch market patterns 24/7.
- Companies use AI to predict cash flow, automate invoices, and price products.

- Credit card companies use AI to detect fraud in real time.
- Amazon and Shopify sellers use AI to write product descriptions, optimize SEO, and test ads.

You may not have millions to manage yet, but you can use the same mindset and tools they do.

Making Money With AI

Once you have a system to manage your money, you can use AI to start **making more of it**:

Ask:

- "What are five online businesses I can start with under $500?"
- "Give me side hustle ideas using skills I already have."
- "What digital products could I sell based on my experience?"

Example: I met a stay-at-home dad who used ChatGPT to outline and publish an e-book on woodworking plans. He made $1,200 in the first month. He reinvested it into tools and now sells kits on Etsy.

Final Thoughts: It's Not Just About Retirement

Wealth isn't only about someday. It's about today.

It's being able to:

- Buy the nicer version instead of the cheapest
- Take your family on vacation without guilt
- Send your kid to college
- Support causes you care about
- Quit the job you hate

You don't have to wait for a perfect moment. Use AI to make a **money moment** happen now.

Let ChatGPT be your **financial thinking partner**. Let it help you ask thoughtful questions, set more substantial goals, and stick to a plan.

Money is power.
And you now have a powerful new way to make more of it.

CHAPTER 5

The AI-Powered Millionaire Mindset

What Rich People Do Differently—And How ChatGPT Can Let You Glimpse Behind the Curtain

Growing Up Between Two Worlds

I was raised in Houston, Texas, in a household that straddled the line between hard-earned comfort and entrepreneurial ambition. My father was a dentist and a visionary—part scientist, part businessman. He was also a man profoundly shaped by contrast.

My grandfather, his father, never finished sixth grade. The Great Depression hit hard, and school gave way to survival. My grandfather spent his life driving oil field trucks, growing vegetables, raising chickens, and living frugally. He didn't believe in life insurance. He believed in land, livestock, and keeping expenses low. Even when they had money, my grandparents still lived like it was 1933. It was how they stayed safe.

On my mother's side, things looked different—but only slightly. Her father had emigrated from Germany, studied engineering at Rice University, and built his own business. He even had patents for oil drilling bits. They had more. They gave more. But they didn't show off. My grandmother sewed her clothes and made my mom's, even though they could afford better. They didn't travel. They didn't splurge. But they were steady, generous, and always had enough.

These two worldviews—one rooted in preservation and simplicity, the other in innovation and calculated risk—collided in my father. He was determined not to live in scarcity. Dentistry, for him, was like printing money. He built his practice not just with skill, but with strategy. He opened his dental labs to lower costs. He studied colors that calmed patients. He adopted dental implants long before most dentists knew what they were.

I spent my early years working in his offices. I saw what success looked like: happy patients, a growing business, and a man who controlled his time and income. We lived in a beautiful home on Memorial Drive and went to Memorial High School, a public school in name but private in lifestyle.

Our classmates wore designer clothes, had their nails manicured weekly, took expensive private lessons, had their clothes tailored to fit their slim bodies, had country club memberships, and had parents who flew first class to Aspen. We didn't always have what they had, but we were close enough to glimpse it—and that mattered.

It showed me two worlds: the wealth you build quietly through discipline and work, and the wealth that opens doors through image, networks, and privilege.

Among my sisters, these lessons landed differently. One acted like a queen from childhood. She expected the best—trips, clothes, experiences—and somehow, she made them happen. She married well, networked like a pro, and lived the ballroom life she envisioned.

Another sister was harsh, transactional. Her goal seemed to be power; she used people to get it. She got rich, yes, but alone, climbing over others.

My youngest sister kept her life close. She worked, married, divorced, and succeeded in quiet ways.

Me? I loved people, making things, solving problems, and building value. Like my dad, I was drawn to entrepreneurship. And like him, I knew that technology—embraced early and fully—was a key to leveling up.

That's what brings me to this chapter: your mindset.

If you didn't go to elite schools, if you weren't born into wealth, if your family wasn't invited to country clubs, don't worry. You have ChatGPT.

You now have a tool that can:

- Teach you the language of money
- Help you plan your future
- Help you look and sound polished
- Suggest wardrobe upgrades for interviews or events
- Draft applications to clubs, schools, or jobs that elevate your life

It's like having an executive coach, stylist, publicist, and financial planner on your laptop.

Social media has helped me stay connected to many high school classmates. I've watched some of them rise through the expected ranks. They married well, stayed slim, and wore that "old money" look. Their kids now attend better private schools than we ever dreamed of. They summered in Europe and wintered in ski resorts.

It used to be that if you weren't born into the circle, you couldn't enter. But things have changed. Today, access can be earned. And ChatGPT is a tool that opens doors.

You can use it to:

- Write cold emails to mentors
- Create social media strategies to grow your business
- Craft proposals for grants, awards, or fellowships
- Learn to speak the language of confidence, affluence, and clarity
- Prepare for meetings, interviews, and events like a pro

In short: AI gives you the millionaire mindset—not in theory, but in tools.

It helps you:

- Think like an investor
- Speak like a leader
- Act like someone already successful

Because success, in many ways, is just a mindset practiced long enough to look like your best life.

You can decide today to level up your mindset. And with ChatGPT, you don't have to do it alone.

Let's build your next chapter—on purpose, with tools, and with wealth in mind.

There's a reason the wealthy stay wealthy—not just income. It's behavior. Mindset. Systems.

Here are 20 things ChatGPT can help you understand, model, and practice that reflect what the wealthy do differently:

1. Create multiple income streams instead of relying on a single paycheck.
2. Track net worth monthly instead of ignoring bank balances until payday.
3. Set long-term financial goals and break them into quarterly plans.
4. Ask better questions about investing, taxes, and cash flow.
5. Hiring professionals or tools to save time—ChatGPT is now one of those tools.
6. Reframe spending into investing (e.g., tools, books, software).

7. Build habits, not just hustle. Wealthy people don't grind 24/7; they delegate, automate, and scale.
8. Understand compound interest and use it to grow savings automatically.
9. Use calendars, reminders, and systems to stay financially organized.
10. Study the markets regularly. Ask ChatGPT for summaries of trends in tech, real estate, etc.
11. Read often. Ask ChatGPT to summarize best-selling finance books.
12. Write goals down and revisit them. Use ChatGPT to help rewrite and adjust as life changes.
13. Speak the language of value. Ask ChatGPT to refine how you pitch your product, resume, or service.
14. Build confidence in negotiations. Practice with ChatGPT before asking for a raise or making an offer.
15. Prepare for key conversations. ChatGPT can simulate a job interview, a grant pitch, or a performance review.
16. Build a wealth-building community. Use ChatGPT to find mastermind or networking groups in your area.
17. Plan travel with reward points. Ask ChatGPT to optimize rewards and cash-back cards.
18. Create a will, living trust, or legacy document. ChatGPT can help outline what's needed.
19. Visualize the life you want. ChatGPT can guide you through vision-boarding and journaling prompts.
20. Think generationally. Wealthy people plan beyond themselves. Ask ChatGPT: "How can I build generational wealth?"

Why Keeping More of What You Make Matters

Wealth isn't about how much you make, it's about how much you keep, and what you do with it.

ChatGPT can teach you how to:

- Identify hidden fees in bank accounts or retirement plans
- Negotiate better rates on recurring bills
- Draft scripts to dispute charges or cancel unused subscriptions
- Create a spending plan that frees up 10% for savings

When you start keeping more, you create **a margin of possibility.** That margin gives you breathing room to invest, try something new, or just sleep better at night.

Building on What You Keep

Keeping more of what you earn is just the first step. The next is letting it work for you.

Use ChatGPT to:

- Draft an email to a financial advisor
- Create a list of dividend-paying stocks
- Compare real estate investment strategies
- Write a one-page business plan for a passion project
- Research passive income streams in your skill area

Think of your money like employees. Don't let them sit idle. Put them to work.

"They were careless people, Tom and Daisy—they smashed up things and creatures and then retreated back into their money..." —F. Scott Fitzgerald, *The Great Gatsby*

We don't want to be Tom and Daisy. We want to be **intentional with money**, not careless with abundance. Having wealth is one thing. Managing it with wisdom and purpose is another.

Inspiration From the Entrepreneurial World

Here's a quote from Richard Branson that always stuck with me:

"Business opportunities are like buses; there's always another one coming."

ChatGPT can help you recognize those buses when they arrive. It can help you:

- Validate ideas
- Assess risks
- Write elevator pitches
- Map your path to your next big thing

You don't need to have an MBA. You need a tool that gives you access to clarity and courage.

So go ahead:

- Dream big.
- Write it out.
- Ask smart questions.
- Build the life you want.

ChatGPT isn't just code. It's your ticket to thinking like the wealthy, acting like the successful, and building a future on your terms.

That's what a millionaire mindset looks like.
And now, it can be yours.

Final Thoughts

Mindset is everything, but a mindset without action is just a wish.

Fundamental transformation happens when you combine the proper perspective with the right tools. ChatGPT can offer clarity, strategy, creativity, support, and the push to finally take the steps that wealthy people take daily.

You don't need a trust fund, a prep school education, or a famous last name to live a life of wealth and abundance. You need intention. You need persistence. And now, you have an assistant that never sleeps, never judges, and is always ready to help you think bigger.

It's not about pretending to be rich. It's about becoming someone who thinks, plans, and grows like someone already is.

And the best part? You don't have to do it alone. Your new success partner is already waiting—right there in your laptop.

Let's keep going. Let's get to work. Let's build the rich life—one smart prompt at a time.

CHAPTER 6

Hustle Smarter, Not Harder AI as Your Productivity Partner

There was a time when hustling meant getting up earlier, staying up later, doing more, and sleeping less. We wore busyness like a badge of honor. We glorified "the grind."

But today? We know better.

Productivity isn't about effort. It's about efficiency.

It's about results, not exhaustion.

And ChatGPT?

It's the ultimate partner in this new era of innovative work.

This chapter is your backstage pass to how AI can help you get more done, feel less overwhelmed, and still have energy left to enjoy your life.

Because the truth is this:

Hustling harder is old school. Hustling smarter is the future.

The Way We Used to Work (And Why It Broke Us)

Let's take a quick trip back in time.

Remember when "getting ahead" meant checking off 50 boxes a day?

You were your assistant, scheduler, note-taker, strategist, editor, and probably part-time snack fetcher. Every to-do list felt like a mountain. Every interruption? A landslide.

I remember once preparing for a product pitch. I spent *days* writing slides, organizing talking points, researching the market, and trying to sound polished. It consumed my brain and most of my good mood.

Fast forward to now:

I can ask ChatGPT, "Give me 10 taglines for this product, summarize the top 3 competitors, write a one-minute pitch in a conversational tone, and include an FAQ for hesitant buyers."

Boom.

It delivers in minutes. I pick what works, polish it, and it's *done.*

That's what working smarter looks like.

That's the *before and after* of AI productivity.

History's Productivity Tools – And Our AI Evolution

Let's zoom out for a second. This isn't the first time humans got a tool that made us faster and more efficient. Just look:

- **The typewriter** saved hours of handwritten notes.
- **The calculator** changed math forever.
- **Spreadsheets** replaced paper ledgers.
- **Google** put an entire library in our pockets.

And now? ChatGPT is the next leap.

It's not just a tool—it's a thinking partner.

You don't just tell it what to do—you *collaborate* with it.

If the calculator made you better at math, ChatGPT makes you better at *everything.*

The Rise of the AI-Powered Side Hustle: Why Now Is the Time to Start

In recent years, the way people earn extra income has transformed. What used to be occasional gig work has now become a **core part of how Americans build financial freedom**—and AI is playing a growing role in that shift.

A national study analyzed search trends for 170 side hustle–related keywords across all 50 states and the 25 largest U.S. cities. The data focused only on search terms showing steady growth over the past three years. The result? Interest in **AI-powered side hustles has increased by 28% in the past year alone**.

Even more surprising is which side hustles are rising fastest. From 2023 to 2024, the top three by growth rate were:

1. **Mobile car wash services** (+276%)
2. **Selling stock photos online** (+151%)
3. **Crypto trading** (+122%)

Other fast-growing options include personal shopping, food delivery, freelancing, online tutoring, and selling digital products.

In cities like New York, Chicago, and Los Angeles, **digital entrepreneurship dominates**—with YouTube monetization leading in New York and Chicago, and crypto trading topping trends in L.A.

So, what's driving the surge? Experts say it's all about **low overhead, flexibility, and convenience**. According to Edward Huang of SideHustles.com, "Customers are looking for services that come to them. Entrepreneurs see mobile car washing not just as a job—but as a business model with minimal costs and high demand."

Another expert, Mark Slack, sees this shift as part of a bigger story. "Side hustles aren't a trend anymore—they're how people are taking control of their finances," he says. "Whether it's detailing cars, selling Canva templates, or filming YouTube videos about something you already know, you don't have to go viral to succeed. Even a few hundred extra dollars a month can make a real impact."

And it's not just a theory. A survey of 2,500 millennials revealed that:

- 52% have at least one side hustle
- 33% juggle four or more jobs at once
- Average side hustle income is $12,689 per year, with some earning as much as $45,000 annually
- While 41% say their side hustle reduced financial stress, 42% also reported burnout
- 58% view "polyworking" (holding multiple gigs) as a sustainable long-term lifestyle

This is where ChatGPT comes in.

AI is making it easier than ever to **start, scale, or support a side hustle**—without needing a business degree or a massive time commitment. ChatGPT can act like your virtual assistant and creative partner, whether you're brainstorming business names, writing product descriptions, creating social media captions, or generating outlines for a digital product.

Getting Started: Small Steps, Big Results

Here's the bottom line: You don't need to wait until everything's perfect to start a side hustle. You just need a starting point—and a few hours a week.

As Slack puts it, "You don't have to reinvent the wheel. Just get on one that's already turning." ChatGPT helps you skip the heavy lifting and go straight to building something real—something that works for your skills, schedule, and goals.

In the next chapters, you'll learn exactly how to use ChatGPT to:

- Test ideas quickly
- Create content effortlessly
- Stay consistent and organized
- Build a personal or business brand
- And most importantly, keep momentum

Whether you're starting with nothing but an idea or looking to turn your side hustle into a full-time gig, **AI is your shortcut to getting there faster**, without burning out along the way.

A Funny Story About AI Productivity (That's Also True)

One morning, I was trying to write a social media caption for a new piece of jewelry I'd made. I had coffee in hand, music playing, the sun coming in the window… and absolutely no idea what to say.

I typed:

"Describe this gold necklace with vintage glass beads in a whimsical, poetic way that fits Instagram."

What did I get back?

"This isn't just a necklace—it's a golden thread of yesterday's elegance woven into today's moment."

I laughed. It was so much better than what I would've written. And my followers loved it.

And here's the kicker: I didn't feel like I *cheated.*
I felt like I finally had a creative assistant who *got me.*

That's how it feels to work with AI at your side.

Now, try having ChatGPT write a poem for you. Here's one it wrote for me to give to you:

The Poem of Productivity

"Ode to the Overwhelmed, Pre-AI Era"

I woke to a list that could crush a strong soul,
A calendar hungry to swallow me whole.
Emails like waves, text pings that shout,
Deadlines that whisper, "There's no way out."

I typed and deleted, then typed once again,
Brain fog thick like a prolonged, slow rain.
Then came a bot, not bossy or cold—
Who answered with wisdom, polished and bold.

Now I prompt, I guide, I let it assist,
It's like having 10 brains—none of which missed.
The hustle's not vanished, but now it feels light,
I sleep like a queen and still ship things right.

Productivity, Transformed: Real-Life Examples

1. The Freelancer Who Bought Her Time Back

Ellie, a freelance designer, used to spend 45 minutes per client proposal. Now, she drafts them in 10 minutes with ChatGPT. She doubled her weekly client outreach—and doubled her income.

2. The Etsy Seller Who Found Her Words

Writing product descriptions used to take forever. Now, she gives ChatGPT the materials and mood, and it writes the listing in her voice. Her sales rose, and so did her confidence.

3. The Life Coach Who Cloned Himself

Jeremy couldn't keep up with the marketing content. With ChatGPT, he drafts emails, repurposes content, and scripts reels. His engagement shot up and so did client signups.

The "To-Don't List": What ChatGPT Can't Do (Yet)

1. Make your decisions
2. Read your mind
3. Fact-check your info
4. Execute tasks (you still have to click "send")
5. Replace human empathy
6. Add personal experience you never share
7. Be your only expert
8. Take action for you

It's powerful. But you're still the driver. ChatGPT is just the supercar.

What's Coming in the Future

- **Talk to it like a friend.** AI will become conversational and context-aware.
- **AI everywhere.** Embedded into apps, calendars, devices—no separate tab needed.
- **Hyper-personalized coaching.** AI that remembers how you work and nudges you accordingly.
- **Team-based AI collaboration.** Brainstorm, organize, and plan with AI in group workflows.

A Tale of Two Days: Before vs. After AI

Before: Exhaustion, overwhelm, repetition, forgotten tasks. **After:** Clear plans, polished writing, creative spark, better sleep. All from *a tiny shift*—working with AI instead of against time.

30 Days of ChatGPT Prompts for Smarter, Faster Success

Day 1:
"What are 10 creative ways to use ChatGPT to grow my business or side hustle?"

Day 2:
"Give me three unique ways to explain what I do for a living—each in a different tone: funny, polished, and poetic."

Day 3:
"Write a checklist to plan a launch for a new product or service."

Day 4:
"Summarize a recent industry trend I should know about in 5 bullet points."

Day 5:
"Help me rewrite my bio to make it sound more exciting."

Day 6:
"Give me a list of 10 inspiring quotes that align with my values."

Day 7:
"Write a warm, professional thank-you email I can send after a meeting."

Day 8:
"Create a meal plan for the week using what's in my fridge: [list ingredients]."

Day 9:
"Give me a new morning routine that helps boost focus and creativity."

Day 10:
"Help me develop five Instagram captions that are funny and engaging."

Day 11:
"Turn this blog post into a YouTube video script." *(Paste your blog post)*

Day 12:
"What are five habits of successful people I can start this week?"

Day 13:
"Create a list of hashtags for my next social media post about [topic]."

Day 14:
"Help me prepare for a difficult conversation by writing out a few scripts."

Day 15:
"Generate three podcast episode titles based on [topic or guest]."

Day 16:
"What are five common mistakes people in my industry make—and how can I avoid them?"

Day 17:
"Help me write a testimonial for a colleague I admire."

Day 18:
"Create an outline for a free lead magnet I can use to build my email list."

Day 19:
"Brainstorm 10 ideas for passive income using my skills in [your skillset]."

Day 20:
"Help me name a new product or service that sounds fun, modern, and clear."

Day 21:
"Draft a pitch email for a collaboration with another brand."

Day 22:
"Write a caption for a 'behind-the-scenes' photo of my workspace."

Day 23:
"Give me a short script for an IG Reel or TikTok on [topic]."

Day 24:
"What's a way to say no to something without burning a bridge?"

Day 25:
"Turn these five bullet points into a polished paragraph." *(Paste your bullet points)*

Day 26:
"What's a creative way to surprise and delight my customers this month?"

Day 27:
"Help me write an elevator pitch that I can use at a networking event."

Day 28:
"Suggest five journaling prompts to reflect on my progress."

Day 29:
"Explain a complex topic I've been avoiding in a way that's fun and easy to understand."

Day 30:
"What's one thing I should do next to get closer to my goals—and how can I start today?"

Final Thoughts

Productivity is no longer about doing more.
It's about doing *better*, with less burnout and more brilliance.

You don't need to wake up earlier, drink more caffeine, or push through exhaustion.
You need a tool that meets you halfway—and pulls you forward.

ChatGPT is that tool.

So, stop wearing stress like it's part of the uniform. Start working like the CEO of your life—with a brilliant assistant who never sleeps.

Hustle smarter. Create more. Breathe deeper.

Your new way of working starts now.

RICH BOT POOR BOT

LET AI MAKE YOU RICH—DON'T BE POOR OR MIDDLE CLASS—FIND YOUR SUCCESS

CHAPTER 7

Networking Like a Billionaire (Even If You're Shy)

We think of billionaires as untouchable. Living on yachts. Hopping on private jets. Walking across stages at tech summits with their sleeves rolled up and their net worth casually ticking higher by the minute.

I have met a few billionaires. Yes, they put their pants on one leg at a time—but they aren't the same as you and me. There's energy around them. Not in a mystical sense, but in a practical one: they walk differently, think differently, and show up in the world expecting success, not hoping for it.

As Dr. Wayne Dyer said, "Abundance is not something we acquire. It is something we tune into." And Esther Hicks reminds us, "You are the creator of your own reality, and so you are not in jeopardy. You do not need to control the behavior of others for you to thrive."

The ultra-wealthy aren't just rich, they've mastered tuning their mindset to wealth. They are often the founders and visionaries behind the brands you know Nike, Microsoft, LVMH, Apple, Amazon, Netflix, Meta, and hundreds of others that span the globe.

Each of those companies started with one or two people with an idea. That idea became a product. That product became a company. And that company became a brand.

The owners and major shareholders of these global brands aren't checking their bank balances, they're watching their *influence* grow. Some are born into wealth, but many built their fortunes from scratch.

Not just with hard work (though that matters), but with *strategy, access, confidence, and connection.*

That's what you're going to learn in this chapter.

Who you know opens more doors than you know.

The wealthiest people in the world aren't necessarily the smartest. But they are:

- *Well-connected*
- *Well-positioned*
- *Well-presented*
- *And incredibly well-practiced at asking for what they want*

How Billionaires Network Differently (And What You Can Copy Today)

Let's break this down. Here's how billionaires network:

1. **They know the value of proximity.**
   - They put themselves in the room. At the conference. In the front row. Not by accident.
2. **They ask better questions.**
   - Instead of saying, "Can I pick your brain?" they ask, "What are you currently excited about in your work?"
3. **They introduce others.**
   - Billionaires are connectors. They don't just network for themselves; they play matchmaker.
4. **They follow up.**
   - The richest people always follow up with a note, a coffee invite, or a small gift. They *remember.*
5. **They speak in value, not need.**

- "Here's how I can help you" is more powerful than "I need this from you."

6. **They don't just build networks, they build ecosystems.**
   - Think beyond LinkedIn. Think co-investors, collaborators, superfans, and advocates.
7. **They treat networking as a strategy, not socializing.**
   - Billionaires don't wing it. They prep like its game day.

What It Means to Build a Billionaire Network

Networking at this level isn't about surface-level transactions. It's not, "What can you do for me today?" It's, "How can we grow something *together* that no one else has thought of yet?"

Billionaire networks stretch across industries, countries, and generations. They sit on boards, attend galas, whisper in back rooms, and text each other about private investment opportunities the public never sees.

Take Bernard Arnault, the head of LVMH and one of the wealthiest people in the world. His luxury empire wasn't built alone. It's a global web of designers, marketers, financial partners, and high-end suppliers. That kind of empire is a *networked masterpiece.*

Or look at Warren Buffett—his famous annual shareholder meeting isn't just about reports. It's about maintaining decades-long trust with other business leaders, investors, and proteges like Bill Gates. Billionaire networking is both legacy-building and opportunity cultivation.

Now here's the secret: **You can do this on your level. Right now.** You might not be in Davos or the Hamptons, but you *can* host your mastermind Zoom call. You *can* start a weekly email circle of value-sharers. You *can* attend community events and ask the questions that get remembered.

You can even use ChatGPT to simulate high-level networking conversations, practicing your presence, polishing your pitch, and preparing for your next big move.

Real-Life Networking Examples from the Wealthy

- **Oprah Winfrey** built her entire media empire not just by talent, but by *relationships.* She championed others, and they championed her.
- **Elon Musk** got significant early funding for Tesla and SpaceX through his PayPal network. Billionaires don't call cold; they friend-call.
- **Sara Blakely**, founder of Spanx, got her product on Oprah's show by hustling and networking through department stores and pitch events. She was a self-made billionaire without a single connection—until she created them.
- **Jeff Bezos** borrowed from friends and family to launch Amazon, then attracted more connections by sharing his vision with everyone who'd listen.

You don't need millions to start networking like this. You need **intention** and **access to the right tools**.

That's where ChatGPT comes in.

Bite-Sized Prompts for Networking Like the 1%

Ask ChatGPT:

- "Write an intro message to someone I admire on LinkedIn."
- "Draft a thank-you email after a networking event."
- "Give me five icebreaker questions to use at a business mixer."
- "Help me follow up after a conference without sounding pushy."
- "Write a short, compelling bio for my speaking gig."
- "Give me ideas for starting a mastermind group in my niche."

Billionaires by the Numbers

- There are about 2,800 billionaires in the world. That's it. Out of 8 billion people.
- The top 1% own nearly 50% of global wealth.
- Over 700 million people live in extreme poverty, surviving on less than $2.15 per day.
- The average Wall Street banker makes over $140,000/year. That's about $70/hour.
- A janitor or cleaner in that same building might make $15/hour or less.
- In the U.S., **1 in 10 homes sold in 2022 were over $1 million**.
- There are **5.8 million U.S. homes worth over $1 million** as of 2023, which is growing.

How Wealth Is Created (and How to Learn from It)

1. **Founding a company**
    - Create a solution to a problem.
    - Build a brand.
    - Scale it. Sell it. Or take it public.
2. **Inventing something valuable**
    - It doesn't have to be revolutionary. It just needs to serve.
3. **Investing in real estate**
    - Buy undervalued. Rent or flip. Compound your gains.
4. **Generational wealth transfer**
    - Inherit property, stocks, and business interests.
    - Manage them wisely or watch them disappear.
5. **Building intellectual property**
    - Courses, books, art, music, licensing.

How Wealth Gets Passed Down (or Lost)

- Some families use trusts, wills, and business entities to keep wealth alive.
- Others lose it within 1-2 generations from poor planning, poor habits, or family disputes.

"The first generation builds it, the second maintains it, the third loses it."

Unless there is *intention* behind the legacy, the story repeats.

Why Networking Still Matters More Than Ever

The world is more connected than ever, but people feel *more disconnected.*

- 85% of jobs are filled through networking.

- Warm intros still beat cold emails by 10 to 1.
- People do business with people they trust, not just the best resumes.

So, whether you're shy, introverted, new in town, or unsure how to start, networking isn't a personality trait.

It's a **skill**. And it's **learnable**.

Use ChatGPT to:

- Practice talking points
- Roleplay introductions
- Draft social media bios
- Help you host your first event
- Create email outreach sequences

The Secret of the 1% Club

Here's what the ultra-wealthy know:

Success isn't solo.

Behind every big name is a list of friends, mentors, advisors, investors, allies, and cheerleaders.

Want to join the club? Build your own list. Grow your network on purpose. Let AI help you get there.

Mini Networking Exercises

1. **The 5x5 Challenge**: Reach out to 5 people you admire this week. Use ChatGPT to help you write short, thoughtful messages.
2. **Gratitude Networking**: Write a thank-you email to someone who helped you professionally—no ask, just appreciation.

3. **Circle Builder**: List 10 people in your orbit who are positive, driven, and creative. Invite them to a monthly Zoom meetup.
4. **Social Media Sprint**: Post one piece of original content daily for five days. Ask ChatGPT to help you brainstorm ideas or polish drafts.
5. **Introduce Two People**: Practice being a connector. Introduce two people in your network who could collaborate.

Case Study: From Freelance Designer to Connector-in-Chief

Tasha was a solo creative working from her spare bedroom. She thought networking meant small talk at boring events. However, things changed when she started using ChatGPT to practice talking points and write connection emails. She launched a bi-weekly email newsletter of curated design tools, and now industry professionals *come to her.*

Tasha used prompts like:

- "Write an email inviting peers to join my newsletter."
- "Help me write a bio that sounds smart but approachable."

She didn't become a billionaire. But she did become unforgettable—and her income tripled in 18 months.

Juicy Fact: What Does It Take to Afford a $1 Million Home?

Let's break it down.

Assuming a 20% down payment and today's average interest rates, here's a rough estimate:

- **Home Price**: $1,000,000
- **Down Payment (20%)**: $200,000
- **Loan Amount**: $800,000
- **Monthly Mortgage Payment**: ~$5,500 (includes insurance/taxes)

What you'd need to earn:

- As a couple: Around **$180,000–$200,000/year** combined (depending on debts)
- Individually: Around **$200,000+/year**, especially with no co-borrower

And you'd need strong credit, cash reserves, and ideally minimal debt.

It's no longer just CEOs or surgeons buying million-dollar homes. In high-cost areas, even mid-level tech workers, social media influencers, and small business owners are doing it, because they:

- Leverage smart loans
- Have passive income
- Run high-margin businesses
- Network their way into opportunity-rich communities

According to Zillow, over 5.8 million homes in the U.S. are now valued at $1 million or more. That means the millionaire housing club is no longer exclusive—it's just *strategic.*

Want one of those homes? Start by:

- **Boosting your income** (hello, side hustle!)
- **Polishing your credit** (ChatGPT can help you write debt negotiation scripts)
- **Learning how money flows** among the ultra-connected

Final Thoughts

You don't have to be born into a powerful circle to build one. You just have to start introducing yourself.

Networking is no longer about cocktail parties and business cards. It's about being brave enough to reach out, wise enough to follow up, and smart enough to use tools that make it easier.

ChatGPT can help you:

- Refine your voice
- Polish your outreach
- Sound more confident
- Be more thoughtful
- And grow your connections like a pro

Because billionaires aren't networking by accident, and neither should you.

Your future collaborators are waiting.

Let the Bot Get You Hired

We all know that applying for jobs can feel overwhelming, especially if you're staring at a dusty old resume and a job market that changes faster than most people can keep up with. The good news? ChatGPT can help you land your next job faster, smarter, and with a lot less stress. It's like having a free career coach, copywriter, and search assistant all rolled into one.

Start with Your Resume

The first step is to give your resume a fresh, AI-powered update. ChatGPT can rewrite your resume to sound more professional, modern, and aligned with your goals. You don't need to be a writer or a branding expert—give ChatGPT the facts, and let it polish your story.

Try this prompt:

"Rewrite my resume to sound more professional. I worked as a retail manager for five years, handling scheduling, hiring, and daily operations. I want to apply for project management jobs."

You'll receive a resume summary and bullet points that sound stronger, clearer, and more aligned with your goals.

Want it to sound like *you*? Add:

"Make it sound friendly and confident, but not stiff or overly formal."

You can also ask:

"Format this resume to work in a plain text email or LinkedIn message."

Find the Right Job Openings

Let ChatGPT help you find job titles you may not have considered. Many people search too narrowly and miss out on great opportunities.

Prompt:

"What job titles are similar to 'community manager' but with better pay or growth opportunities?"

Or ask:

"What remote job options exist for someone with experience in customer service, writing, and scheduling?"

You can even ask it to generate example companies or industries you hadn't thought of.

Then, when you find a real job post you like, this is where ChatGPT shines.

Tailor Your Resume to Match the Job Description

This is the secret sauce. Most hiring software scans for keywords from the job description. If your resume doesn't include them, a human may never see it.

Paste the job listing into ChatGPT with this prompt: "Here is a job I want to apply for. Can you rewrite my resume bullets and summary to match the keywords and tone of this listing?"

Let the bots do the heavy lifting.
Your next job could be one prompt away.

Add your resume content and the job post in the same message. ChatGPT will analyze the description and highlight skills, values, and keywords the company cares about, then update your resume accordingly.

You can also say:

"Make my resume match the job description without exaggerating or making it sound robotic."

ChatGPT can also help write your cover letter, LinkedIn headline, or email to the hiring manager. All of it can be customized to reflect *your* personality and goals.

Quick Wins: Get Job-Ready Fast with These Prompts

- "Summarize my experience in three bullet points that sound confident and professional."
- "Write a short cover letter based on this job post and my resume."
- "List 5 questions I should ask during a job interview for this role."
- "Write a thank-you email to send after an interview for this job."

The job market favors the prepared; now, with ChatGPT, you can be one of the best-prepared people out there. This isn't cheating. It's collaborating with a powerful tool to put your best self forward.

Turn Messy Notes into Meaningful Content with ChatGPT

If you're staring at a page full of chaotic notes and thinking, "Where do I even begin?"—you're not alone. Your ideas might be brilliant, but when they're jumbled, it's hard to find the good stuff. That's where ChatGPT can help.

With just a few simple prompts, you can transform a notebook full of half-thoughts into a clear, organized, and usable outline. Whether you're building an article, presentation, social media plan, or creative project, these prompts will help you move from overwhelm to structure—fast.

Step 1: Let ChatGPT Extract the Gold

Start by giving ChatGPT all your unfiltered thoughts. Then use a prompt like this:

Prompt:

"Write up the text from this image. After that, analyze my notes and extract the five most important ideas or themes. For each key point, provide a brief

explanation of why it appears significant—based on repetition, context, or emphasis. Then create a clean, organized outline that I could use as the foundation for an article, presentation, or project plan."

This lets you skip the grunt work of deciphering your own scribbles and go straight to developing your best ideas. Focus your energy on creating, not reorganizing.

Step 2: Categorize Scattered Ideas into Clarity

If your notes feel random and disjointed, ChatGPT can help sort them into useful categories. It's like turning a messy junk drawer into a tidy toolbox.

Prompt:

"Review this image of my handwritten notes and categorize everything into clear, logical groups. Create a table with three columns: Category, Key Points, and Potential Applications. For each category, identify the main concepts from my notes and suggest how I could develop them into content. Then recommend which category would be the strongest starting point for creating valuable material."

This process not only helps you see your ideas more clearly, but it also shows you **where to start**—and starting is often the hardest part.

Why This Works

You don't need to be a master organizer to turn notes into something great. With the right prompts, ChatGPT does the heavy lifting so you can focus on **refining, writing, and building**. Your ideas deserve to be seen—this is how you bring them to life.

Let's go say hello.

CHAPTER 8

The Power of Side Hustles — Build Wealth While You Sleep

There has never been a better time to start a side hustle. Technology has lowered the barrier to entry. AI has leveled the playing field. Social media gives you a direct line to customers. And most importantly, people just like you are doing it every day, sometimes turning $100 into six-figure incomes in just a year or two.

Side hustles are no longer a hobby. They're the new resume. They're the backup plan that becomes the primary plan. And they're one of the fastest ways to start building wealth from wherever you are, with whatever you have.

Whether you want to make an extra $500 a month or build a brand that could sell for millions, this chapter is for you.

Real Story: From Late Nights to Lightbulb Moments

Let me tell you about Rachel. She was a teacher in her mid-30s, a single mom scraping together just enough to cover daycare, bills, and the occasional treat. She loved her job, but her paycheck said otherwise. So, one night, she stayed up Googling, "How to make extra money from home." Sound familiar?

She found an idea: digital planners. She didn't know a thing about Etsy or Canva or how to design a digital product. But she was determined. With the help of YouTube videos, some free templates, and ChatGPT to write her product descriptions, she uploaded her first planner.

It made one sale in the first week. Then three. Then twenty.

She kept learning. Added more products. Created a simple email list. Six months later, her planner shop earned enough for all her daycare costs. A year in? She took a trip with her son to Disney World—and paid for the whole thing with planner money.

She still teaches, but now she teaches with options she built with her own hands and a little help from technology.

Stories like Rachel's remind us that side hustles aren't just about the hustle. They're about the *hope* that comes with taking back control.

Why Side Hustles Matter More Than Ever

- They build financial freedom.
- They reduce your dependence on a single employer.
- They let you explore your creative side.
- They become testing grounds for new business ideas.
- They are recession-resistant (people still spend money on value and entertainment!).

And now, with AI like ChatGPT, you don't have to do it all alone.

You can:

- Brainstorm product names
- Write marketing copy
- Create email newsletters
- Plan a launch timeline
- Draft responses to customers
- You're no longer the only employee. You've got backup.

Quick Hustles vs. Long Game Wealth

Quick Hustles are great for generating fast cash:

- Selling digital downloads
- Pet-sitting
- Freelance writing
- Reselling thrifted items on eBay or Poshmark
- Long Game Hustles focus on asset-building:
- Building a niche blog or YouTube channel
- Launching a product brand
- Creating an app or online platform
- Investing in real estate or dividend stocks

Savvy entrepreneurs do both. They start with cash flow, then reinvest in long-term vision.

30 Side Hustle Ideas Ranked (Easiest to Hardest)

EASIEST (Start today)

1. Sell printables on Etsy
2. Flip garage sale finds on Facebook Marketplace
3. Offer pet sitting or dog walking
4. Sell baked goods or snacks locally
5. Do simple graphic design with Canva
6. Become a virtual assistant
7. Sell digital resume templates
8. House-sit or babysit
9. Sell custom crafts or jewelry
10. Offer lawn care or yard cleanup

MODERATE (Takes some setup)

11. Launch a blog and monetize with affiliate links
12. Create a niche YouTube channel
13. Design T-shirts with print-on-demand sites
14. Freelance on Fiverr or Upwork
15. Sell online courses or eBooks
16. Launch a social media management service
17. Host local art or maker workshops
18. Build a subscription box service
19. Run an Airbnb from your home or guest house
20. License your photos or illustrations

ADVANCED (Long-term potential)

21. Start a digital marketing agency
22. Create a mobile app or SaaS tool
23. Develop and flip niche websites
24. Publish a book series or intellectual property
25. Start a branded product with wholesale partnerships
26. Launch a coaching or consulting program
27. Import/export niche products
28. Buy vending machines and manage them
29. Invest in short-term rental properties
30. Buy a small business and grow it

Think Bigger: Business Principles to Guide Your Hustle

- **Solve a specific problem** — Niche wins every time

- **Validate before you build** — Ask your audience what they want
- **Outsource early** — Hire others for design, writing, and shipping
- **Track your time and revenue** — If it's not growing, shift your strategy
- **Reinvest your profits** — Buy better tools, ads, or start a second stream
- **Build a brand, not just a business** — Make it memorable
- **Collect emails** — Email lists are digital gold
- **Systematize** — Create repeatable workflows
- **Know your numbers** — Profit margin, cost of goods, ad spend
- **Play the long game** — Plant seeds you'll harvest for years

Build a Side Hustle Army

What if you could build a side hustle—and not even be the one doing all the work?

Welcome to the delegation model:

1. Hire a virtual assistant for customer service.
2. Outsource your packaging and shipping.
3. Bring on a freelance designer or copywriter.
4. License your knowledge to others and earn passively.

Your side hustle becomes a *business*, and then a *brand.* And before you know it, you're hiring others while focusing on strategy.

Always Be Learning: Who to Follow for Ideas

Great entrepreneurs share their side hustle wins on Instagram, YouTube, and even TikTok. Follow people like:

@CodieSanchez (buying boring businesses)

@TheBudgetnista (money tips and side income ideas)

@JustinWelsh (solopreneur content creation)

@ErikaKullberg (legal tips and creator monetization)

@HustleNation or @SideHustleStack (curated side hustle lists)

And my favorite, Chris Koerner @thekoerneroffice

Also, watch what's trending in Forbes, Business Insider, and Fast Company. Many of the most innovative side hustles aren't coming from Silicon Valley—they're popping up in small towns, rural villages, and online communities worldwide.

When you follow these creators, the algorithm starts serving you more ideas. It becomes a nonstop feed of potential businesses.

ChatGPT-Powered Hustle Planner

Use prompts like:

- "Help me validate an idea for a candle business."
- "Draft a landing page for my art class side hustle."
- "Write five ad captions for my new jewelry line."
- "What should I charge for editing services based on market research?"
- "Create a checklist for launching a digital product."

Let ChatGPT handle the busy work, so you can focus on what matters: launching, selling, growing, and *thriving.*

Side Hustle Discovery Worksheet

Use this worksheet to help identify a side hustle that fits your life, goals, and talents. You can write your answers in a notebook, journal, or note-taking app.

Step 1: Know Yourself

- What skills do I have that people ask me for help with?
- What hobbies or passions do I love enough to spend weekends doing?
- What experiences have I had that others would find valuable?
- Do I enjoy working alone or with others?
- How much time can I commit to a side hustle per week?

Step 2: Define Your Goals

- Why do I want to start a side hustle? (Extra cash? Escape my job? Test a business idea?)
- How much money do I want to make each month?
- Am I looking for quick income or long-term growth?

Step 3: Evaluate Your Resources

- Do I have tools (laptop, camera, car, sewing machine, etc.) to help me get started?
- What startup funds can I invest ($0, $50, $500)?
- Who do I know that could help me get this off the ground?

Step 4: Match & Test

- Which three ideas from the "30 Hustles" list most excite me?
- What's a straightforward way to test each one in the next seven days?
- What did I enjoy most, and what felt like a drag?

Step 5: Take Action

- Circle one idea you're going to commit to.
- Write the first three steps to launch it this week.
- Use ChatGPT to draft your plan, script, post, or first offer.

Remember: you don't have to get it perfect. You just have to get it going.

Final Thoughts

A side hustle isn't just about extra money; it's about owning your time, talents, and future. Whether you're selling your first handmade bracelet or mapping out a full-scale business empire, every single step counts.

You don't need a trust fund. You don't need a fancy office. You need grit, curiosity, a bit of structure, and the belief that you can create something valuable.

Start small. Stay scrappy. Reinvest your wins. Keep showing up. And when do you need help? You've got AI in your corner now.

Your side hustle might start in your kitchen or garage, but it could take you worldwide.

Big dreams love bold action.
And your next one is just a prompt away.

CHAPTER 9

How AI Understands Wealth, Value, and the Power of Wanting More

Let's start with something tangible.

Wanting more money, more time, more success—isn't shallow. It's deeply human. It's how we survive. It's how we grow. It's how we dream. The desire for abundance is older than any financial system. It lives in our instincts, our stories, and our goals. And today, thanks to tools like AI, we can finally make more of those dreams a reality—faster and smarter than ever before.

We must be clear when discussing AI and money: AI doesn't "want" anything. It doesn't crave a paycheck. It doesn't feel ambitious. But it *understands* what we do. AI is trained on the entirety of human knowledge, from spreadsheets and bank statements to TED Talks and self-help books.

It knows how we think about wealth, how we chase it, how we fear losing it, and how we talk ourselves into or out of believing we deserve it.

It understands that for many people, money represents:

- Freedom
- Security
- Status
- Power
- Possibility

AI sees money as patterns. It reads how we describe financial goals, analyze risk, and make purchasing decisions. And when you ask the right questions, it can reflect that understanding back to you—and even make you more innovative with your behavior.

Let's explore how.

How AI Can Help You Understand Your Relationship to Money

Try asking ChatGPT:

- "Help me identify my money mindset—am I an avoider, hoarder, spender, or investor?"
- "What are five common beliefs that hold people back from building wealth?"
- "Create a plan to shift from scarcity to abundance thinking."
- "Write three journal prompts about money and self-worth."

Money isn't just math. It's emotional. And AI can guide you into reflection, clarity, and action—if you use it as a tool for insight, not just output.

Narrative: The Shift in My Thinking

There was a time when I believed money came from showing up, working hard, and doing good work. That's it. That was the formula.

But the world changed. I saw people making money through courses, content, digital products, investments—doing work once, and getting paid repeatedly. They weren't smarter than me. They just thought differently. They asked different questions.

When I started using ChatGPT, I noticed something. The more I asked about wealth, success, and mindset, the more I began to think it was better. It wasn't just a tool. It was a mirror. It helped me see what

I wanted, how other people got what they wanted, and the words, confidence, and strategy to go after it myself.

It didn't make me rich. But it made me *ready*.

And that's the first step.

What AI Sees That You Might Miss

AI has access to millions of examples of:

- How the wealthy spend their time
- What successful entrepreneurs invest in
- The habits of high-net-worth individuals
- Market trends and behaviors that build momentum
- Which industries are growing and which are shrinking

It sees what works. It knows what's been tried. It recognizes patterns we don't see because we're too close to our own lives.

Want to build wealth? Ask your AI assistant questions like:

- "What are the habits of people who build wealth by age 40?"
- "What investments are best for someone starting late?"
- "Compare the pros and cons of starting a business vs. freelancing."
- "Explain how compounding works and how to start today with $100."

Global Perspective: How the Desire for Wealth Looks Around the World

Billions of people worldwide want more, but their definitions of "more" vary.

- Over 700 million people live in extreme poverty, earning less than $2.15/day.
- In the U.S., the median household income is around $75,000/year.
- A $1 million net worth places you in the top 1% globally.
- In cities like London, Dubai, Singapore, and San Francisco, there are growing communities of ultra-wealthy individuals who built their wealth from tech, real estate, media, and global trade.

AI studies everything: the pain, the drive, the systems, and the success stories. It learns from every angle.

So can you.

Using AI to Pursue Value, Not Just Money

Money is great. But real wealth is valuable: the ability to create, contribute, and grow something that matters.

Let AI help you:

- Define what value you offer
- Clarify your message to the world
- Build systems that make your work easier to share
- Launch products that solve real problems

Final Thoughts

AI doesn't feel hungry. But it understands our hunger to succeed.

It can't want more—but it knows how we do.

So, use it. Ask it more profound questions. Challenge yourself to grow. Let it remind you that wealth isn't a mystery. It's a pattern. It's a strategy. And it's possible.

Not someday.
But starting today.

CHAPTER 10

Money Talks, AI Listens—Using AI to Build Wealth

We all want to make our money grow, but most of us were never taught how. Financial literacy often feels like a secret language, reserved for the elite or the ultra-nerdy. And traditional financial advice can feel cold, complicated, or completely disconnected from real life.

But AI? It listens. It learns how *you* think, what *you* value, and how to guide you toward better money habits and smarter decisions—without shame, confusion, or overwhelm.

In this chapter, we'll explore:

- How the wealthy think about money differently (and how to adopt their mindset)
- How to use AI as your personal finance guide and virtual money coach
- Real examples of people using AI to budget, invest, and grow their wealth
- A list of AI tools that help you manage, track, and multiply your money

Get ready. Your money is about to start working for *you*.

More Real-Life Wins: AI + Everyday People = Wealth on Purpose

Case 4: The Six-Figure Earner Who Still Felt Broke

Natalie made over $120K/year at a big marketing agency—but spent every dime. She used ChatGPT to analyze her spending patterns and asked for tips on automating her savings. Within a month, she set up three sinking funds and invested in fractional shares. "I finally feel like my money is working for me," she said.

Case 5: The Retiree Learning Late

Charles, 68, never thought much about tech. But his granddaughter showed him how ChatGPT could help organize his retirement income. It helped him build a basic spreadsheet for pensions, IRA withdrawals, and expenses. "It's like a financial secretary that doesn't sleep," he joked. Now he uses it weekly.

Case 6: The Young Hustler with a Vision

Diego, 22, wanted to travel but also save for his future. He asked ChatGPT, "How can I split $1,000/month between savings, investing, and fun?" The bot helped him create a simple 50/30/20 plan and suggested apps to automate it. He's now saving for his first trip to Thailand and investing confidently.

Reflect + Rewire: Money Mindset Prompts

Use these questions to break out of old thinking and into wealth-building clarity:

- What money beliefs did I grow up with—and are they still serving me?
- Do I believe I can be wealthy? Why or why not?
- When I think about rich people, what words come to mind?
- If I had all the money I wanted, what would I *really* be doing?

- What's one financial habit I'm proud of—and one I'd like to change?

Try asking ChatGPT to help you turn those answers into:

- A personal money affirmation
- A weekly money goal
- A step-by-step plan to build new habits

Mini Worksheet: Your Wealth Action Plan

1. What is your current monthly income?
2. What are your three main financial goals right now? (e.g., pay off debt, save for travel, start investing)
3. What tools or habits are you currently using to manage money?
4. What's one area where you feel stuck?

   Let ChatGPT help you with:

   - A script to call your credit card company
   - An investment comparison
   - Budget categories
   - Passive income ideas based on your skills
5. What bold action will you take this week to grow your money mindset?

Around the World: How AI Is Changing Wealth

- In **Nigeria**, young entrepreneurs use ChatGPT to start online businesses, from digital art to content writing.
- In **India**, coders and educators use AI to create exam prep tools and language tutoring businesses.

- In **Brazil**, creators use AI to write social media captions, grant applications, and business plans in English.
- In **Germany**, professionals use ChatGPT to simulate salary negotiations and write investor emails in multiple languages.

Wealth looks different in every country, but AI brings the *tools* closer to everyone.

What the Rich Teach Their Kids That the Poor Don't—And How AI Can Now Teach You

In *Rich Dad, Poor Dad*, Robert Kiyosaki introduced two fathers: one who taught him to chase security, and one who taught him to build wealth. But today, many people don't have either voice guiding them. That's where AI can step in—not as a replacement for real mentors, but as a third kind of teacher. The one you didn't know you had, available 24/7.

Kiyosaki taught that the rich buy assets, not liabilities. That they work to learn, not just to earn. They need to understand taxes, leverage, and systems. You can now use AI to:

- **List all your liabilities and convert them into assets**
- **Learn how different business entities affect your taxes**
- **Simulate investment scenarios with various returns and timelines**
- **Draft scripts to talk to accountants, advisors, or lenders**

You may not have grown up with a rich dad. You may not have been taught how money works. But now you have access to something no generation before you ever had:

An AI that learns with you, thinks with you, and supports your wealth journey—without judgment.

The original *Rich Dad* message was: *You can learn to be rich.*

The updated message in *Rich Bot, Poor Bot* is: *You can learn to be rich, and now you don't have to do it alone.*

Final Vision Exercise: Why You Want Wealth

Close your eyes and answer this:

- If money were no longer a problem, what would your life feel like?
- What kind of person would you become?
- Who would you help?
- Where would you live?
- How would your days look?

Now, ask ChatGPT:

"Help me write a personal wealth vision statement in one paragraph."

Print it. Post it. Speak it. And start living it.

Because now, you have the tools.
Now, you have the knowledge.
And now, you have the momentum.

RICH BOT
POOR BOT

LET AI MAKE YOU RICH—DON'T
BE POOn OR MIDDLE CLASS—
FIND YOUR SUCCESS

CHAPTER 11

Brand You – How AI Helps You Build Authority

Everyone has a brand. You don't have to be a celebrity or a social media star to have one. Your brand is your reputation, and what people say about you when you're not in the room. It's the energy you carry, the words people associate with your work, and the feeling you leave behind.

Today, your brand is one of your most valuable assets. And AI? It just became your brand-building partner.

In this chapter, we'll explore:

- Why building a personal brand matters in any field or stage of life
- How AI can help you define, express, and grow your brand presence
- Real examples of people using AI to build audiences, launch products, and grow reputations
- Tools and templates for amplifying your voice, style, and message

This is where visibility meets credibility—and AI helps you scale both.

Coming next: narrative, templates, brand strategy prompts, and a guide to turning your voice into your advantage.

Why Building a Personal Brand Matters

Whether you're a freelancer, an employee, an entrepreneur, or someone just exploring what's next, your brand tells the world what to expect from you. It's how opportunities find you. It's how people remember you. It's how your name becomes a recommendation. In a crowded digital world, your personal brand isn't optional— it's your calling card.

It builds trust. It opens doors. And when it's done right, it works for you even when you're asleep.

How AI Can Help You Define, Express, and Grow Your Brand

AI takes the heavy lifting out of branding. It helps you:

- Define your niche and voice through writing prompts
- Polish your messaging for different audiences
- Create visuals that match your brand identity
- Maintain consistency across all platforms
- Generate endless ideas so you never run out of content

From building your mission statement to writing your About Me page to practicing your elevator pitch, AI can mirror your voice, reflect your values, and help your identity shine.

Real People Using AI to Build Their Brands

Eva, *The Wellness Coach*

Eva used ChatGPT to help structure her messaging, write her email campaigns, and create content calendars for Instagram. She also trained a custom GPT with her coaching methodology so new clients could get instant onboarding.

Marcus, *The Voiceover Artist*

Marcus used AI to create a portfolio website, generate his marketing copy, and practice mock interviews. Within six months, he landed three national brand gigs.

Tanya, *The Etsy Seller*

Tanya sells handmade bath products. She used AI to write her listings and SEO descriptions and create automated customer replies. Her conversion rate doubled within 90 days.

AI didn't replace their voice. It *amplified* it.

Tools + Templates for Your Brand Growth

Here are tools (and AI prompts) to help you express your voice and style:

- **ChatGPT** — For bios, emails, captions, headlines, brand story
  - Prompt: "Write a 3-sentence brand story for a [job title] who is [adjective, mission]."
- **Canva Magic Write / AI** — For visual branding, mood boards, templates
  - Prompt: "Design a brand mood board using calming earth tones and minimalist fonts."
- **Notion AI** — For organizing brand goals, content calendars, and mission planning
  - Prompt: "Create a weekly planner that includes content, client outreach, and time for skill-building."
- **DALL·E / Midjourney** — For brand imagery, product mockups, visual storytelling
  - Prompt: "Generate a modern logo for a tech-savvy, creative jewelry brand."

- **Descript / ElevenLabs** — For podcasting, video scripting, voiceovers
    - Prompt: "Write a 60-second voiceover script introducing my new podcast about creative entrepreneurs."

These tools give your ideas form, voice, and reach without requiring a design degree or an expensive agency.

You're not just building a brand. You're building trust, connection, and visibility.

And now, you have the smartest co-creator on the planet helping you make it real.

Your AI-Powered Roadmap to Success

The fastest way to success isn't about doing more—it's about doing the *right* things, consistently.

Your AI assistant is the ultimate productivity partner: always ready, available, and focused on helping you level up. This roadmap is your daily toolkit for building your personal brand, making smarter decisions, and creating long-term wealth.

Every action in this checklist is designed to:

- Clarify your message
- Strengthen your identity
- Save you time
- Multiply your results

Use this system to build clarity, consistency, and confidence one habit at a time. Don't try to do everything at once. Pick one or two actions that fit your season, and let AI do the heavy lifting for you.

Below you'll find:

- Your **Brand You** checklist for daily brand growth

- **5-minute wins** to build smart habits fast
- Weekly systems to check in, level up, and move forward
- A final 30-day challenge to turn all of it into momentum

This is how you become known, trusted, and in demand—without burning out or breaking the bank.

Whether you're a freelancer, coach, small business owner, or professional with something to say, these daily practices build the scaffolding of your brand over time. You don't need a massive following. You need clarity, consistency, and courage. AI helps you bring those to life, day by day.

Use this checklist as a creative accountability partner. Each item is a practical daily prompt to help you clarify your voice, strengthen your brand presence, and use AI to save time while growing your influence. You can work through it one task daily or repeat it weekly to build momentum.

Brand You: Daily AI Checklist

- (You fill this out with your bot)

Simple Daily Habits to Build Wealth, Make Smarter Decisions, and Work Less

5-Minute Daily Wins with AI

- (You fill this out with your bot)

Weekly Wealth Habits

These habits are designed to help you stay in tune with your financial life and make course corrections in real time. AI allows you to review trends quickly, ask smarter questions, and make informed decisions faster than ever.

- (You fill this out with your bot)

Weekly Wealth Habits (Expanded)

- (You fill this out with your bot)

These simple habits compound. And when guided by AI, they take less time but get sharper results. Use this system weekly to stay grounded, grow steadily, and adjust with clarity.

This is your future—and you just made it brighter.

CHAPTER 12

The Future of Success—Why AI Will Shape the Next Millionaires

This amazing time we live in

In the digital age, information is power, and when it comes to money, knowledge can make the difference between surviving and thriving. One of the most influential and transformative ways to use ChatGPT is to improve your financial literacy. Whether you're budgeting, investing, planning for retirement, or getting out of debt, ChatGPT can be a 24/7 companion on your journey to financial freedom.

Why Financial Education Matters

Financial education isn't just about numbers—it's about freedom. When you understand how money works, you gain the power to make choices that align with your goals and values. You stop being reactive and start becoming proactive. You learn how to make money work for you, rather than vice versa.

Unfortunately, most of us were never taught about compound interest, emergency funds, or how to analyze a credit score. But the good news is: it's never too late to learn.

Using ChatGPT for Personal Finance

Here are just a few of the things ChatGPT can help you with:

- **Budgeting Help**: Ask it to create a monthly budget based on your income and expenses.

- **Debt Repayment Plans**: Get tailored advice on tackling student loans or credit card debt.
- **Investment Basics**: Learn the difference between ETFs and mutual funds or ask it to explain risk tolerance.
- **Side Hustle Ideas**: Brainstorm realistic ways to earn extra income based on your skills.
- **Understanding Financial Terms**: If a word like "APR" or "dividend yield" makes your eyes glaze over, ask ChatGPT to break it down like you're five.
- **Retirement Planning**: Even if you're just starting, you can use ChatGPT to understand IRAs, 401(k)s, and long-term planning.

Keeping the Curiosity Alive

Financial education isn't a one-and-done topic. The more you learn, the more empowered you become. Use ChatGPT to stay current with new trends like cryptocurrency, sustainable investing, or interest rate changes. Ask it to explain news stories, compare financial tools, or even help you role-play as an investor or entrepreneur.

Encouragement for the Journey

Don't get discouraged if it all seems overwhelming. Start where you are. Ask one question. Learn one concept. Take one small action. The quest for financial knowledge and freedom is lifelong, and it pays dividends beyond dollars.

You don't need a finance degree. You need curiosity, consistency, and a tool like ChatGPT to support you. Keep going. You're building a future where you understand and control your money, instead of your money controlling you.

Exercise: Your AI Future Roadmap

Reflect on your business or personal career path and identify opportunities for AI integration.

1. **Assess Your Current Status**
   - What technologies or processes are you currently using?
   - Where do you notice inefficiencies or gaps?
2. **Identify AI Opportunities**
   - Which of the AI-driven opportunities listed resonate most with your goals?
   - How might they directly impact your work or life?
3. **Set Clear Goals**
   - Write down three achievable goals for integrating AI into your activities.
   - Create deadlines for implementing each goal.
4. **Measure and Adjust**
   - Plan how you will evaluate the success of each integration.

Goal, AI Tool/Platform, Deadline

Goals	AI Tool/Platform	Deadline
Example: Improve customer service	Zendesk Answer Bot	Within 3 months

Commit to regular check-ins to assess your progress and adjust accordingly.

Completing this exercise will give you a clear, actionable roadmap to harness AI for future success.

CHAPTER 13

The World is Changing Fast—How to Stay Ahead

The pace of technological innovation has never been faster. To stay relevant, you must continuously anticipate what's next and embrace lifelong learning. Adopting AI isn't just wise—it's essential.

The Most Significant AI-Driven Opportunities Coming Next

AI is no longer limited to automation; it's evolving into a cornerstone of creativity, business intelligence, and decision-making. Emerging trends include:

- **Generative AI for personalized products** – Customize experiences, products, and services effortlessly.
- **Advanced AI-driven marketing analytics** – Predict customer behavior with pinpoint accuracy.
- **AI-enhanced education** – Tailor learning journeys to individual strengths and weaknesses.
- **AI in healthcare** – Precision medicine, predictive diagnostics, and telemedicine platforms.
- **Sustainability and climate-tech AI** – Tools for optimizing resources, managing environmental impacts, and innovating renewable solutions.

Why Early AI Adopters are Already Winning

Businesses and professionals embracing AI are capturing market share rapidly because they're:

- More responsive to market changes and customer needs.
- Efficient in resource allocation, significantly reducing costs.
- Leveraging predictive analytics to outsmart competitors.

Consider Amazon's AI-driven recommendation engine, Tesla's autonomous vehicles, or Canva's AI-powered design tools—all examples of early adoption generating massive competitive advantage.

Quick Wins: How to Future-Proof Your Success with AI Today

- **AI-Powered Writing Tools:** Jasper.ai, Writesonic, and Grammarly Go for generating high-quality content efficiently.
- **Business Intelligence Platforms:** Tableau AI, ThoughtSpot, and Microsoft Power BI to make informed, data-driven decisions.
- **AI-driven Customer Service:** Intercom, Zendesk Answer Bot, and Ada.ai for automated customer interactions.
- **Financial Planning and Investment:** Wealthfront, Betterment, and Robinhood's AI-driven analytics for smarter investing.
- **Learning and Personal Development:** Khanmigo (by Khan Academy), Duolingo's GPT integration, and Coursera's personalized AI-learning tracks to sharpen skills continuously.

By exploring these tools and platforms, you position yourself among forward-thinking people already leveraging AI to redefine success and shape tomorrow's wealth. The future isn't just coming; it's here, driven by those who embrace AI today.

Final Thought: The Real Bot Is You

Let's bring this full circle.

If you've read this far, you've spent the last 112 pages learning how to use ChatGPT to get answers and to ask better questions, spark ideas, and build something real. You've seen how a few well-written prompts can unlock creativity, streamline your life, and maybe even jumpstart a side hustle.

So, here's the truth behind the Rich Bot / Poor Bot concept: it's never really about the bot.

ChatGPT responds to your curiosity, follows your direction, and amplifies your intentions. In other words, your success isn't determined by the tool; it's **determined by the mindset of the person using it.**

A "Poor Bot" is just a missed opportunity. A rushed prompt. A thought that never made it past the surface. A copy-paste approach to something that deserves originality.

But a "Rich Bot"? That person sits down with a sense of play, focus, and possibility. Someone who's not afraid to try, to test, to tweak. A Rich Bot doesn't have all the answers—it knows how to start asking better questions.

And that person? That's ***you.***

You've already taken the most important step: **you showed up with curiosity and stayed with it long enough to learn.**

My hope is that this book gave you more than tips and tricks—it gave you a new lens on what's possible. Whether you're starting a business, writing your story, organizing your world, or simply experimenting with something new, ChatGPT can be the partner you didn't know you needed.

But the real magic? That's you, choosing to show up. Choosing to create.

FINAL CHALLENGE

30-Day AI Success Challenge

Build your AI muscle and your future with this light, fun, and doable challenge:

Week 1: Clarity + Confidence

1. Ask AI to summarize your strengths
2. Write your mission statement
3. Draft 3 bios
4. Brainstorm 10 content ideas
5. Generate a daily plan
6. Create a list of dream clients or jobs
7. Build a vision board with AI image prompts

Week 2: Brand + Business

1. Define your niche or audience
2. Write an elevator pitch
3. Create a weekly content calendar
4. Write your first newsletter or post
5. Pitch yourself to be a guest on a podcast
6. Map your first product or service 14. Identify one skill to start monetizing

Week 3: Wealth + Wellness

1. Set a monthly savings goal

2. Use AI to plan your grocery budget
3. Create a passive income brainstorm list
4. Ask AI to explain investing basics
5. Draft your retirement wish list
6. Create a time-blocking schedule
7. Ask AI to write your perfect workday plan

Week 4: Momentum + Mastery

1. Automate one business task
2. Write a thank-you note or testimonial
3. Analyze your social media growth
4. Roleplay a sales conversation 2
5. Ask AI for feedback on your messaging
6. Draft a landing page or product pitch
7. Identify your next big goal
8. Break it into five action steps
9. Celebrate what you've built—and plan your next prompt

Keep learning. Keep prompting. Keep going.

You've got this.

"An investment in knowledge pays the best interest." – Benjamin Franklin

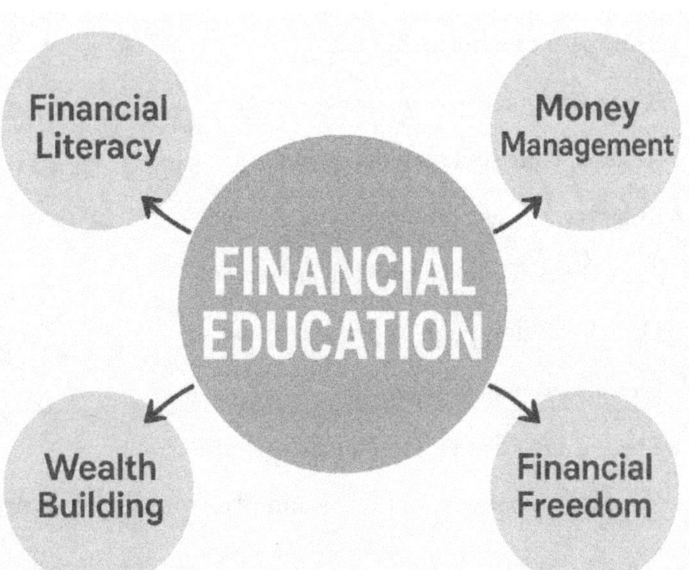
Financial
Literacy
Money
Management
FINANCIAL
EDUCATION
Wealth
Building
Financial
Freedom